ANGELIQUE CHAPMAN
RICO GRADY
HOW FAR WOULD YOU GO TO HELP A STRANGER?
Mile 19
WWW.HOWARDCLAYFILMS.COM
"MILE 19"
BUFFALO 8 AND HOWARD CLAY FILMS IN ASSOCIATION WITH MARK FEATURES
EXECUTIVE PRODUCED BY: MATTHEW HELDERMAN LUKE TAYLOR RABESHIA CLAY ANDREA PAUL HOWARD CLAY JR.
MUSIC BY: JULIAN JOHNSON DIRECTOR OF PHOTOGRAPHY: CHRIS ORR EDITED BY: NICOLE BAER PRODUCTION DESIGNER: ANDREA PAUL
STARRING: ANGELIQUE CHAPMAN RICO GRADY VIVIAN GIL ASSIA LAU'REN EUANTON DOTSON JEROME JOHNSON
PRODUCED BY: RABESHIA CLAY WRITTEN AND DIRECTED BY: HOWARD CLAY JR.
HOWARD CLAY FILMS
buffalo 8
A BONDIT COMPANY

the *Publisher's* Desk

I have never been as excited as I have been over this past month. Not only did I see my dream come true with the first print edition of B.O.S.S., but I was able to witness so many of my friends' and colleagues' children graduate! What a wonderful experience! We see so many negative images of African-Americans and minorities every day. From internet videos to news reports, we are flooded with images that are not positive. But this month on Facebook, Twitter, and every other social networking site, I've seen more rewarding, encouraging, and amazing stories than I ever had. I don't want just one month of the year (and maybe February), where people are excited about education and progressing forward for our community... I want B.O.S.S. to go into the homes of everyone and encourage our youth all year, every month.

I believe being positive is contagious. I believe promoting and supporting positivity is key to a change happening in our community. We can not continue to look for "someone else" to fix our community, it has to start with us. Small steps. Small things like changing what we read, changing what we watch, and changing what we listen to. Finally change what we support. We have to make education, a priority, not an option.

Our first issue has done well, but let's keeps this momentum going! Share with your friends, family, coworkers, doctor's office, churches- wherever they need education is where we want to be. The future is clear; B.O.S.S. eMagazine is the future of urban magazines for minority youth! Thank you for your support, now enjoy the issue!

Howard J. Clay/ Publisher

Howard J. Clay

Howard J. Clay is available for speaking engagements, clinics/ seminars, as well as appearances for organizations, corporate and school events.

For Booking
howardjclay@hotmail.com

Editor's Note

First, and foremost, thank you all for subscribing, buying, picking up, and supporting the first print issue of B.O.S.S. last month and making our print debut a success! Tell a friend to tell a friend to tell their sister, cousin, uncle twice removed to do the same this month.

Now, on to business...

Honestly, I had no idea what to write for this issue. Writer's block is an actual thing. None the less, here I am with a message of thanks, encouragement, and motivation topped with a quirky, funny dash of personality (at least I hope so).

Congratulations to the 2014 graduating class!!! No matter what level in school or life you have completed this season, you have succeeded in progressing your life to the next level. Be it a job, a new school, a new life lesson, a new friend, whatever, you are embarking on a new journey. Here's a pat on the back for not only making it this far, but for wanting to go further!

While I didn't graduate from school myself this spring, I did make it out of Biology 2 and Chemistry 2 in one one piece! For those of you who don't know, I am a post-baccalaureate pre-med student. This is a fancy way of saying I went back to school after graduating college to complete the medical school pre-requisites. Along with this, I am currently pursuing a Master's of Business Administration in Marketing. Talk about a full course load! This summer I am starting the Organic Chemistry sequence and I am scared and excited and nervous for what the future brings. I know most of you are feeling the same way about your own journeys. At this point, all I can tell you is to use that excited energy state and jump in! I know I am!

I applaud you for pushing through when everything seemed to be going wrong. You didn't give up... That determination will help you continue through the next stage. You can do it and I am along with you for this ride! Let's get going!

As always, continue to be your own success story... You've done it this far! Congrats!

-Andrea

@Drea_Elizabeth

Andrea Paul
Editor-In-Chief

Andrea Paul is available for speaking engagements, clinics/seminars, as well as appearances for organizations, corporate and school events.

For Booking
drea@boss-emag.com

B.O.S.S. eMAGAZINE Staff

Board of Directors:

    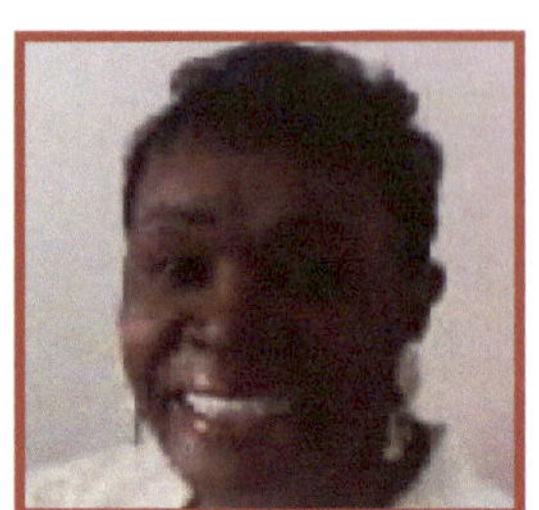

Martin T. Shepherd, Esq. EQT Corporation

Dr. Adrienne Booth Johnson CEO Infinity Global Connections

Aisha Felder Principal Marketer of Red Shoe Marketing Group

Tiffanny Harden-Evens Esq.

Chaplain Linda Clay

Founder/Publisher
Howard Clay Jr.

Co Founder/Editor in Cheif
Andrea Paul

Art Director
Emmanuel Johnson

Editorial/Digital Content Manager
Cierra McClurkin

Marketing and Advertising Manager
Desha Elliott

Media Relations Manager
LaTresa "Tree" Cunningham

Promotions Director
Jeffrey "Royce" Clay

Contributing Writers:
Lindsay Harper

Travis Jackson

Sia Knight

Marcia Franklin Robinson

Terra Couzins

Brad Allen

Tiffany Hall

Shaneen Murray

Contributing Editors:
An Howard

Linda Clay

Cover Photo Credits:
Nebula Arts

www.Nebulaarts.com

Special thanks to: Short Run Printing Ltd, Hope Finney, Dr. Jackie Walters, Eboni Cummings, Lakesia Ross, Melinda Santiago, Nicci Gilbert, Angel McCoughtry, Dr. Adrienne Johnson, Derek Anderson and Terry Boehmker.

Thank You!

BLACK HISTORY Facts

"I believe that each of us comes from the creator trailing wisps of glory."

"I am a Woman
Phenomenally.
Phenomenal Woman,
that's me."

"I've learned that people will forget what you said, people will forget what you did, but people will never forget how you made them feel."

"You may not control all the events that happen to you, but you can decide not to be reduced by them."

"My mission in life is not merely to survive, but to thrive; and to do so with some passion, some compassion, some humor, and some style."

"The need for change bulldozed a road down the center of my mind."

"Try to be a rainbow in someone's cloud."

"I've learned that you shouldn't go through life with a catcher's mitt on both hands; you need to be able to throw something back."

"We may encounter many defeats but we must not be defeated."

"You are the sum total of everything you've ever seen, heard, eaten, smelled, been told, forgot - it's all there. Everything influences each of us, and because of that I try to make sure that my experiences are positive."

"One isn't necessarily born with courage, but one is born with potential. Without courage, we cannot practice any other virtue with consistency. We can't be kind, true, merciful, generous, or honest."

"Love recognizes no barriers. It jumps hurdles, leaps fences, penetrates walls to arrive at its destination full of hope."

"Nothing can dim the light which shines from within."

"Never make someone a priority when all you are to them is an option."

"We allow our ignorance to prevail upon us and make us think we can survive alone, alone in patches, alone in groups, alone in races, even alone in genders."

"If you don't like something, change it. If you can't change it, change your attitude. Don't complain."

"Nothing will work unless you do."

"History, despite its wrenching pain, cannot be unlived, however, if faced with courage, need not be lived again."

"You may not control all the events that happen to you, but you can decide not to be reduced by them."

"One isn't necessarily born with courage, but one is born with potential. Without courage, we cannot practice any other virtue with consistency. We can't be kind, true, merciful, generous, or honest."

"I've learned that you can tell a lot about a person by the way (s) he handles these three things: a rainy day, lost luggage, and tangled Christmas tree lights."

"Ask for what you want and be prepared to get it."

"A bird doesn't sing because it has an answer, it sings because it has a song."

"The honorary duty of a human being is to love."

"Try to be a rainbow in someone's cloud."

"I love to see a young girl go out and grab the world by the lapels."

"I've learned that people will forget what you said, people will forget what you did, but people will never forget how you made them feel."

Inside B.O.S.S.

18

B.O.S.S.
eMAGAZINE
Substance In Every Issue

June 2014

One

Section 1

1st

First

If you think college is a scary thought for some high school students, imagine being the "1st First"!
What is the "1st First"? It's the first child from a family who is the first to go to college. Schools and scholarship committees call these youth,
"first generation college students."
For a lot of minority high school students this is an unfamilar reality.
In this section, you will always find advice and articles to help make the transition to college a little easier for our 1st Firsts.

Luke 12:48 says, "From everyone who has been given much, much will be demanded." In order for a woman to be at boss status, she must know her responsibilities and be prepared to put her best foot forward at all times. Now, when I say "boss status" I don't mean boss as in supervisor, I mean boss as in a woman who makes major moves! A boss woman is confident in herself and the decisions she makes. She is intentional and always thinks things through. She's a provider and a nurturer. She's highly respected and admired by all. A boss woman can be a mother, an executive, a friend, a mogul... she can be you.

When I think of a boss woman, one person who comes to mind is Ms. Tyra Banks. Tyra has made the most of her life and career and she continues to take it to another level. She took what made her successful- modeling, and paid it forward by turning it into an opportunity of a lifetime for aspiring models all over the world. She has built a pretty impressive empire too. Now, that's what I call bossy!

Not all of the women I call a boss are well-known or famous. I've had the pleasure of being in the company of several boss women and heroines throughout my life. These women are a part of my bloodline. When I think of strength, poise and grace, I see the faces of the beautiful women in my family. I think of my great-aunt who was a young bride and adopted three children before she finally had one of her own. Even while raising her four children, her home was always open to her nieces, nephews and grandchildren. She has selflessly helped raise fifteen children but only gave birth to one! Now you'd think someone like that would never have bad luck, but even when life reared it's ugly head (death, betrayal by her natural child, starting over at 70) she handled it all gracefully. That's what I call a boss.

I see my mother's face when I think of a boss woman. After giving birth to me she, was devastated to learn the doctor's accidentally gave her a hysterectomy and at age 19 she could no longer have children, literally killing her dreams of giving me a brother or sister. Over the years I've watched her

go through many phases, the ups and the downs... she's quite complex, but her strength is amazing. The delicate flower I call mom is truly the biggest boss that I've seen thus far.

The list of boss women in my family is long. From a cousin who raised her younger brothers while their mom was on drugs to becoming a police officer who chased thieves, successfully, ran a side business, attended film school, and picked up the pieces to her grandmother's perfect puzzle. They were the glue that helped keep their families stuck together.

Only a woman of boss status can manage all of that. To be a boss woman, you must be willing to smile and stand tall even in the midst of pain and trouble. You must be willing to make power moves whether the world is watching or no one is watching, whether everyone knows your name or no one knows your name. A boss is a leader and she's prepared to take on ANY task that is put before her. She's all about accomplishing and has no time for things of a petty nature. A boss does what she has to do but she doesn't rob Peter to pay Paul, she holds her own at all costs. She's creative and inventive, always thinking ahead. A boss is proud but she is not prideful, she's secure enough to ask for and accept help from others when it's needed. She's honest with both herself and everyone else, there's no room for lies. Before she'll use you to help her, she'll use herself to help you. A boss woman is an authentic woman.

Being a boss is about more than making millions of dollars or dictating rules, it's about leadership and humility. Anyone can call themselves a boss, but do they display boss-like qualities? That's what a real woman of boss status does, she talks the talk and she walks the walk! "From everyone who has been given much, much will be demanded." Are you ready to be a boss?

Don't Knock the Hustle!

-Tiffany Hall

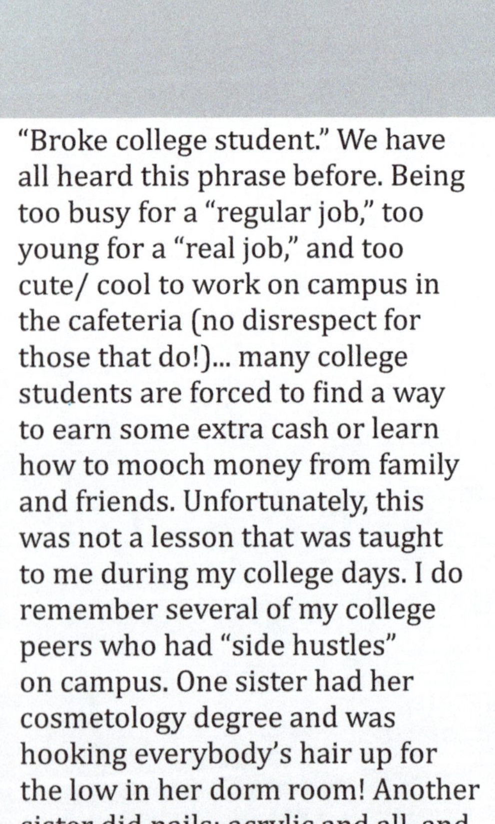

"Broke college student." We have all heard this phrase before. Being too busy for a "regular job," too young for a "real job," and too cute/ cool to work on campus in the cafeteria (no disrespect for those that do!)... many college students are forced to find a way to earn some extra cash or learn how to mooch money from family and friends. Unfortunately, this was not a lesson that was taught to me during my college days. I do remember several of my college peers who had "side hustles" on campus. One sister had her cosmetology degree and was hooking everybody's hair up for the low in her dorm room! Another sister did nails; acrylic and all, and yet another sister braided hair. While the rest of us were barely getting enough money to eat off campus, they were getting paid! Why didn't anybody tell me that I needed to have a hustle while I was in school? In hindsight I wish someone had told me to make sure that before I left home, I had some kind of hustle that would put money in my pocket!

It wasn't until 6 years after I'd graduated from college that I became a "hustler". My first exposure to being an entrepreneur was as an Independent Beauty Consultant with Mary Kay Cosmetics. Being in that company opened my eyes to so many things! It taught me business skills, personal skills, speaking skills, and most importantly, it taught me that if you need to make a dollar or two, you had the ability to go out and make it happen! I will be forever grateful for my MK experience. To this day, if I need some "extra" money, I know how to "hustle" it up. Do you need $20 to go to that frat party this weekend? Why not sell some clothes that you don't wear anymore to Plato's Closet? Hustle! Need some cash to pay that initiation fee into that sorority/ fraternity? Why not offer baby-sitting services to local families (only if you are good with children, please) or mow someone's lawn (elderly people would love to pay someone else to do that for them)? Hustle! Do you need a couple of dollars in your pocket every month, if for no other reason, than just to not be a broke college student? Then Hustle!

Now hustling does come with responsibility! Your hustle must be

legit! No illegal hustling! Your hustle must not interfere with your education. You are your own B.O.S.S., so set a schedule that works for your school schedule. Your hustle should be funded by you, if at all possible. When you get that fat student loan refund, instead of blowing it on clothes or partying, invest it into your hustle. Lastly, your hustle is just that-- a hustle! Unless your life's goal is to be a professional hair stylist or to run your own landscaping business, do not let your hustle take precedence over your real life goals! Now get out there and make some money!

Here are just a few ways that you can get your hustle on:

• Selling items on EBay, Selling clothes to consignment shops
• Hair (styling, braiding, cutting)
• Tutoring
• Nails
• Lawn services
• Network Marketing Businesses (Mary Kay, ACN, Avon, Zamzuu)
• Kids' Birthday Parties (face painting, tattoo artist, balloon maker, photographer)

Are Some Students Really Turning Down $10,000 for College?

S.I.A Knight

During the beginning of each year, many families are making decisions about what college to choose. It is also the time when paying for college becomes a reality.

I recently spoke to a good friend of mine who was frustrated because she works in a large school division and she was concerned that there were not enough applicants for a very lucrative local scholarship.

In her area business owners in the community pool their resources each year and offer a $10,000 scholarship to be awarded to a local student. There is no GPA requirement for this award, the requirements just specify that the student show academic merit and demonstrate need. It also specifies that the student be involved in some type of community service and be a U.S. Citizen.

Can you guess how many students had applied by the deadline? Out of the 12,000 high school seniors enrolled in that school system, the scholarship committee had received 14 applications. For $10,000 scholarship! This blew my mind, so much so, that I had to research this myself. I was sure that my friend had left out some important details. Surely students were not prepared to leave $10,000 on the table. I searched and the opportunity was properly advertised in the school system's database and on individual school websites.

This was so shocking that it made me revisit a post that I wrote previously on my blog at Siaknight.com entitled - Why Are Students Skipping the Scholarship Search?

I searched through some of the rationale in my previous post for a reason why the students may not have applied for this lucrative award:

The first reason that students don't apply for enough scholarship money is that they don't know how –Some students are totally unplugged from the college preparation process, this includes knowing where and how to find and apply for scholarship money.
This is particularly true for first generation college students. Unfortunately,many of them miss out on

"… In the end, the bottom line is that if only 5% of the students in the senior class applied for the scholar-ship…"

money that they may qualify for simply because they are "out of the loop". It is imperative that we as mentors, advisers and counselors push these students to seek private financial assistance and clearly articulate the message that completing the FAFSA isn't enough.

I recognize that it can be extremely difficult to ensure that students are fully taking advantage of the resources that are available to them. However, I believe that we as educators have a duty to direct students to all possible opportunities

Students will often tell advisers that their GPA or test scores aren't high enough to pursue scholarships. Not true! Many organizations award scholarships based on a number of criteria independent of grades or test scores.

This group includes students who are fortunate enough to have parents that were able to save enough money to fully fund their college education and others who have scored sizable university scholarships. These students have the mistaken notion that they don't need to seek outside sources of money. The fact is that incidental costs like travel and school fees can cause a tremendous strain for families who fail to plan for these hidden expenses. Outside scholarship money can help to fill in the gaps.

The last reason that students don't apply for enough scholarship money is that they are unwilling to do the work that it takes to apply for the awards.
On numerous occasions, I have seen many scholarships go to the candidates who simply bothered to write the requisite essay. I know that senior year in particular is very busy for high school students but, we as counselors and advisers must stress the importance of carving out time to apply for private scholarships. Believe it or not, I have heard of some students who are "turned off" if a contest is only awarding $300 or $500. If an essay takes 2 hours to write, I often advise, a $500 scholarship will earn the winner $250 per hour! When put in those terms, two hours seems like reasonable investment of time.

 In the end, the bottom line is that if only 5% of the students in the senior class applied for the scholarship, readers would have had over 500 to choose from. Instead, committee members had to make their selection based on 21 applicants.

This has to change.

Do you know of a young student that:

***Displays excellent character**

***Outstanding behavior**

***Positive attitude towards others/ learning**

***Good citizenship throughout the year**

***Demonstrates responsibility**

***Respectful to peers/teachers**

***Follows classroom/school rules and expectations**

Please TELL us about them in a 300 word essay and submit it to editor@ boss-emag.com

We would love to highlight a young education success story!

STUDENT OF THE MONTH

Allow me to introduce to you
Ms. Morgan Heard,
B.O.S.S. eMagazine's student of the month!
She is the 3rd oldest child of 9, six brothers and two sisters, whom she makes proud every day. Morgan is a 2014 graduating senior from Fort Zumwalt North High School in St. Louis, Missouri where she played softball and basketball. When I asked her what obstacles she has faced being a student-athlete she said, "Time management is my biggest problem, but it will always be my studies before sports because if I don't study and get good grades I can't play sports." She wants to set the example for her younger siblings that school is important no matter what they want to be in life, and she has certainly proven that with her list of awards. Morgan received and Academic Plaque for maintaining a 3.4 GPA or higher for 7 or more semesters, a College-Prep Certificate, and an Essence of PPI Award. She plans to continue her education at Southeast Missouri State University (SEMO) where she will be double majoring in Elementary and Early Childhood Education with an Autism Certificate. She received a John Wells Memorial Scholarship, an Alpha Kappa Gamma Scholarship, and Residence Life Leadership Scholarship to accompany her there. Morgan hopes to continue her softball journey as a lady Redhawk! This is just one of her many goals.
 Morgan has plenty of goals set for herself as she begins her post-secondary journey. One of which is to be on the Dean's List and keep good grades as she did in high school. She is full of hope, vigor and inspiration, and hopes the same for her peers. When asked what her advice is to students who don't know what they want to do after graduation is, she said, "At least try, go to community college for a year, and see what your passion is because it's always good to have a college degree under your belt." Join myself and B.O.S.S. eMagazine as we congratulate our student of the month, Morgan Heard!

-by Nikole Kane

Spelman College

A Choice to Change the World

Spelman College, Atlanta, GA
Spelman is one of the nation's top liberal arts colleges. Considered the unofficial "sister school" of Morehouse College, this all- female, private, HBCU provides students with a number of opportunities to get involved on- campus and in the Metro- Atlanta area!

- Quick Facts
---- Estimated Price Tag: $32,474 including tuition, fees, and room and board
---- Undergraduate Population: 2,177
---- Type of Institution: Private
---- Mascot: Jaguars
---- School Colors: Blue and White
---- Founded: 1881 as Atlanta Baptist Female

- Who Went Here
---- Mattiwilda Dobbs Janzon: First African-American to perform opera at La Scala
---- Varnette Honeywood: Artist and Creator of the children's book character "Little Bill"
---- Shaun Robinson: Actress and Correspondent for television show "Access Hollywood"
---- Keisha Knight-Pulliam: Actress known for her childhood role as "Rudy" on "The Cosby Show"

- Top 5 Subjects to Study
---- Biology
---- Psychology
---- Political Science
---- English
---- Economics

- Get Involved
---- Submit your own research proposal or join a project through the Office of Research Resources.
---- Apply for a Co-Op experience with some of the most notable companies in Downtown Atlanta.
---- Join one of the 6 sororities at Spelman, including the 4 National Pan-Hellenic Council member organizations.
---- Attend the Women of Color Conference to engage with other Spelman women and

- Ready to apply? Visit www.spelman.edu for more information.

** All information is made available through the Spelman College website. Additional information can be obtained from the National Center for Educational Statistics at
www.nces.ed.gov.

Dr. Jackie Walters

Married to Educating

Dr. Jaqueline Walters, M.D. is the tell-it-like-it-is, face making reality TV star we have all come to love. Even in a relaxed environment, the doctor in her has a voice. An advocate for patient education, higher education, and living an optimistic healthy lifestyle, Dr. Jackie, as she is so fondly known by her patients and fans of the Bravo TV show Married to Medicine, mixes profound knowledge with her inviting attitude. Here, B.O.S.S. had the chance to sit down with the busy physician and learn more about her journey in medicine, both as a doctor and as a patient.

B.O.S.S.:What made you want to be an OB/GYN (obstetrician/ gynecologist) or a physician in general?

Dr. Jackie: I don't know if any of you have been from a small town, but there they don't really use proper terminology and they don't tell you exactly what you need to know. The female anatomy had a different name... everything had a different name (referring to medical diseases and anatomy). I kept saying to myself from age 8, "when I grow up I want to be able to help little black girls understand being a female. I'm going to go to medical school and I'm going to tell them about being a woman." Also, [OB/GYN] is a "well-woman" field and it's a relatively happy one. We smile a lot, we laugh a lot, and we see mostly happy things on a regular basis. It's not heart disease; it's not asthma; it's not hypertension. We don't see patients come in with a long list or a bag of medicines they've been prescribed. It's a happy field, most days.

I left Fayette, Mississippi, a small town, thinking that I couldn't do this because when I was young I never saw doctors who looked like me. The first time I saw one, was when I had wen to Meharry [Medical College] for a visit. I was like, "oh my gosh, a black doctor!" (Laughs.) In Fayette, we had one here or there, but seeing a whole population of black doctors... you just didn't see it. So I thought becoming a doctor was unattainable.

I knew that the only way out of that small town for me was through education. I went to college thinking I would just do a medical technician program. I'll be in medicine, but not really in it. Then, I got to college and thought, "these people are not as smart as me. I can do this." ...And here we are.

Why specifically OB/GYN instead of Maternal Fetal Medicine, or either obstetrics or gynecology?

Maternal- Fetal is an additional two, three years of training and you also lose the surgical part aspect of practicing. I like operating. Rarely in Maternal-Fetal Medicine will you cut a patient or perform surgery. In OB/GYN, I get the "gyn" side where I will take out fibroids, take out a uterus... It gives me more diversity with women, whereas in MFM, you will just deal with pregnant women with issues.

What would you say to students who say that the path to becoming

a doctor takes too long?
I would say that there are "seasons" to this. You're in college and having fun and it's great. Then, there is medical school… Even though you are in medical school, you can still have a great life. Yes, there are periods of study, study, study, but then you will have periods of good times. Your classmates will become your family since you are around each other so much in medical school. Then, you have residency and during residency you get paid- you get a check. It's not a lot of money, but you have a job and a check while you are still studying. It's delayed gratification… studies show that people who have delayed gratification have been linked to greater intelligence. A person who works hard now can play hard later. They may see the big houses and cars, but they don't see the many nights I am up late. They don't see that I have a tremendous amount of work to do. No one sees that part. They just see the gratification. Work hard, it pays.

What was your motivation and passion for educating young black women? Is it because you are a black woman?
My being a black woman is important, but also so much of the things I didn't know growing up, I was shocked to find out. So, I lived by scripture "in all your getting, get an understanding." [Proverbs 4:7] If you understand WHY as a patient, it is much easier to have them comply. For instance, if you walk in and ask, "why do I need a breast exam, why do I need this?" I will tell you that by the time you palpate a lesion on your own, you are already at stage two. So, it's much easier to treat you if we find it early than having you find it yourself. [Patients] will go to the doctor and say, "I don't want to do anything about it, I just wanted to know why." They do it all the time. This is why we see women with fibroids that look like they are 30 weeks pregnant. They knew they had them, but they didn't want to do anything about them. I do this to educate… to have patients understanding the facts. People just want to know why. If you let the patient feel like the copilot, they are much happier. I do remind them sometimes whose name is on the door, but for the most part they are the copilot.

Tell us more about your fight with breast cancer.
I had no family history. None of the risk factors you read on the list

"The leading cause of death in African American women is heart disease…"

I had… except not having a baby. When I got that first diagnosis, I wanted to ask why me, but then I said, "why not me." I felt that I was equipped to handle it. Statistically, they said I had a 3% chance of ever having this again, you're good. So, I'm proceeding with life, planning a baby, a car, picket fence, good job- I'm good. The second diagnosis was a bit much to handle for me. As a woman, the things that we cherish the most, we lose in breast cancer. Your hair, your breasts, your femininity is distorted from the whole breast cancer journey. Plus, I knew too much.

I have a book called Both Sides of the Knife, and in it I want people to hear the story from the layperson's and from the physician's perspective. As soon as they said "cancer," I wanted to know what were the lymphovascular spaces,

if there were mitotic figures in the pathology… I just knew too much to ask. It made it hard because they didn't' always give me the answers I wanted to hear. So, it was a little tough. Now, it has created a whole sense of knowing that you can't fight this journey without tears. So cry and get it over with, but know that it is a fight.

50 Shades of Pink started because when I was in chemotherapy I thought it was important to go to chemo looking cute! (Laughs.) It's a morbid setting were you go into this big place and everyone is hooked up to IV's with televisions on in the background and they have scarves on that didn't match their clothing. …and who would notice that? No one but me! I wanted to buy everyone scarves. I'd tell them if you put this scarf

on you can put it to the side, put a bow here, and just look cute. Well… I got pulled out of chemo and they put me in the conference room because I was too busy going up and down the lane, telling people, "unplug your pump you can go to the bathroom." Then I got in trouble for giving people tips on how to finish the day's treatment quicker so we could leave sooner. (Laughs.)

I couldn't do treatment with the others, but I always dressed up and did the whole makeup thing. I wanted to cry the night before because you knew that afterwards you were going to feel horrible, you wouldn't be able to taste anything, and that you couldn't smell for about 7 days. I just felt that if you went in there dressed cute, the experience would be more bearable. I would always

"I can't stop being a physician..."

Photo credit: Jeff Photography

give that advice to women who were diagnosed [with cancer]-- dress up! Go get a nice, inexpensive outfit and wear it to chemo. The people who did treatment with me would always dress up and we would go out right after and eat. I sat in treatment thinking I looked good and it worked for me.

Do you have any advice to women who seem to lose their identities in the disease instead of coming out of it and staying positive?

I just lost a friend who had been battling it 3 years, and we have two other ladies who have been given time limits for this year. For one of the women, this is her 5th reactivation of the cancer in the past 5- 6 years, but she remains super positive. She would take chemo, the cancer is gone, the CT is clean, and then it returns. The other, who got diagnosed about

1½ years ago, has never gotten better and she's angry. Your attitude is your altitude. We know, medically speaking, you immune system is so much stronger when you are happy. Your white blood cells and endorphins fight for you. When you are sad, you secrete cortisol and insulin… everything that creates damage to the body. If you want to take it from a spiritual standpoint, be happy, it works. I always tell patients after I deliver the diagnosis or they come in to see me, "let's cry." We cry one good time and get it out, but then I ask, "what are we crying for? Because you're going to lose your hair? Because you don't want this to be you? Tell me what we are crying for." They need to know why, but from there on if they understand the exact process of what is going to happen, then it all seems like

a piece of cake. I thought oral boards (Medical Licensing Exam Step 2) was worse than chemo! (Laughs.) Your attitude is going to make a difference. Your attitude determines your chemical makeup. What is good health and what does it mean to be healthy?

Good health is more than physical health; it's mind, body, and spirit. We did the motto "Fit is the New It" and we used "fit" instead of thin or skinny because "fit" encompasses your body and mind and your spirit. So being healthy is a person who is whole mentally and physically. Last year, I got dubbed, "thin is in." Thin has a negative connotation to it… If you tell someone to be thin, they can take it too far, all the way to anorexia. I wanted to let people understand that when I said thin, I meant fit. To make sure the word

"I saw something recently that said you have two paths, and no matter which path you take, you still have to deal with the consequences."

got out we changed it to fit is the new it. One- third of America is obese and 82% of African-American women are obese based on a BMI (body mass index) of 30. So, being fit is now a minority. I'm watching my father struggle with Alzheimer's. He had diabetes and hypertension and refused to manage it. I think him not controlling those diseases led to small vessel disease, poor profusion to the brain, and now has Alzheimer's. Unfortunately, I really think that he had a part in it. For the younger generation, we believe that a portion of you will be deaf because you always want things to be loud, just like [the older generation] loses their sight after a certain point of maturity. We are now finding autism in the uterus and there are tests that can tell if your baby is at risk for autism. It's the stimulation, or lack thereof in my dad along with him not taking care of himself. [Health] is like a car. When you buy a new car you take excellent care of it for a year, then you start to buy bad gas and throw trash in it, and you look up and realize that car doesn't last 10 years. You get what you invest in. If you invest in your health now, in the long term, you will do much better.

What advice would you give to our readers?

I saw something recently that said you have two paths, and no matter which path you take, you still have to deal with the consequences. I think if young people understand money, education and especially health, you can have all the money in the world, but if you're sick, you are just a sick man with money. Health is your greatest wealth. We go back to delayed gratification; you don't always have to have fun. That will come.

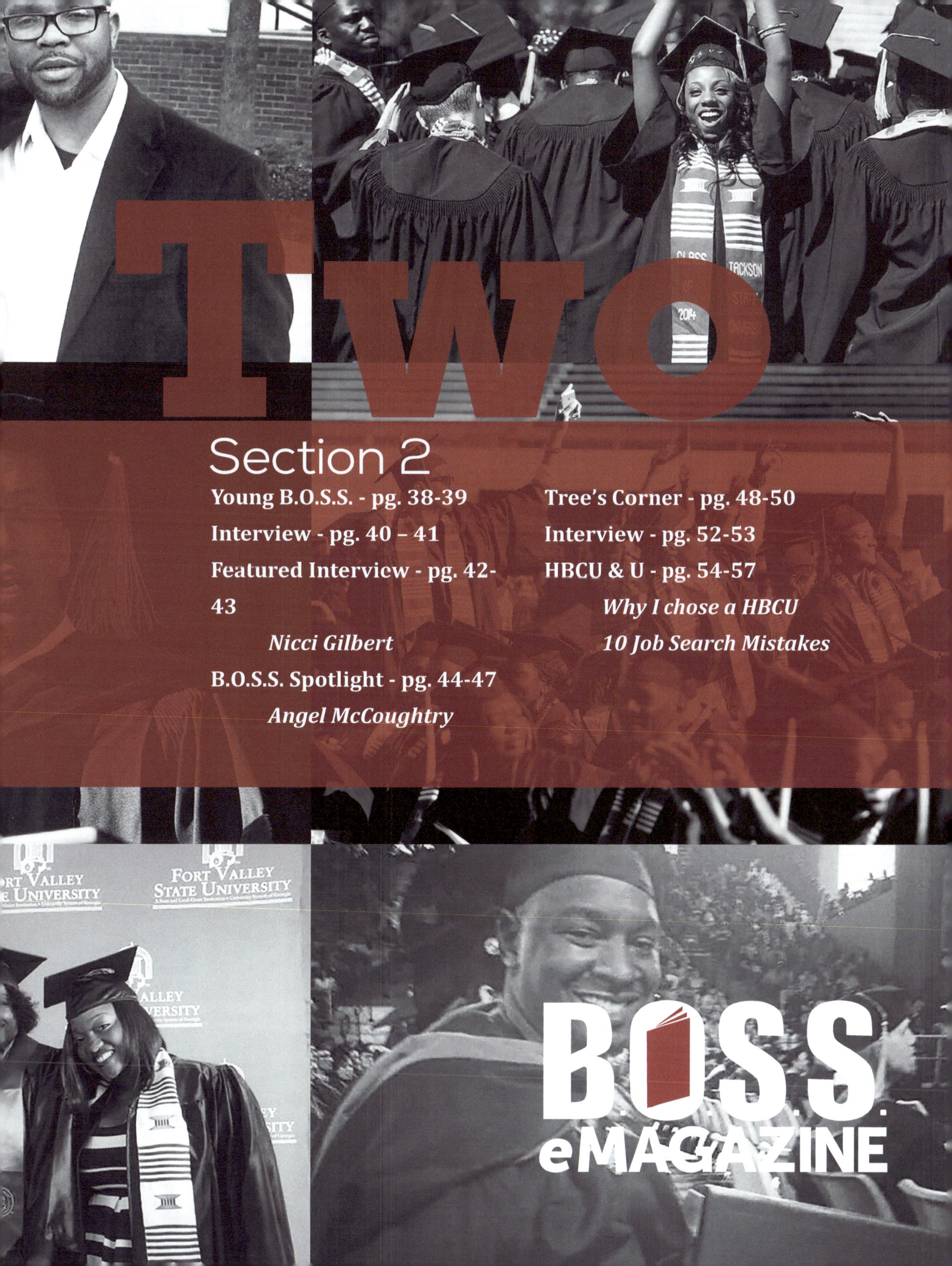

TWO

Section 2

B.O.S.S. eMAGAZINE

What do you do when what you're doing isn't your passion? Meet Jean Catherine. A mechanical engineering graduate of Western Michigan University currently working in the manufacturing industry who is ready to make a change to follow her dreams of becoming an interior designer.

Jean
Catherine
Follow your passion

B.O.S.S.: What made you change your career from manufacturing to interior design?
Jean: Interior design has been on my mind for quite some time actually. When I was a child, I liked rearranging my room in different ways… setting up the plans, mapping out a picture to scale, and moving everything by myself. The best feeling was showing my dad and brother what I had done and seeing the look on their faces. I went to school for mechanical engineering because it was more practical. It was a way to be able to support yourself when you got into the real world. Interior design didn't seem practical at that time. Now, I am in my field, I am making money, and I am basically successful. I'd like to start working and putting my efforts towards something that would make me happy.

When you were a child, was there anything else you thought about doing as an adult?

I wanted to go into theater. In school, I was in the drama club. I was in all the school plays and had leading roles. It was fun to learn my lines and become a different person on stage. To me, that was a route that was even less practical than interior design, so I stayed with engineering.

Besides income and security, what gave you the motivation to step out of practical and go for your dream?
I was never motivated by money, which is odd by what I previously said. I just wanted to be independent. Now that I am, I have the means to finally pursue my passion. It's not money that I am driven by. People would say, "this job can help you make such and such amount of money and do well." and I would ask if it would make me happy. So now that I am financially stable, I am going to put all my effort into making sure that I am successful and

"The biggest obstacle that you'll have to face is yourself. You are the ruler of your fate."

happy with what I do.

So up until now, what has made your passion for interior design persist over time?
I would say research has kept the passion alive. I am getting more involved in learning what the industry is like and sketching my ideas. I have a developing passion for furniture and would like to become a furniture designer. Right now, I am getting ready to go back to school. UCLA has a graduate program where a bachelor's in interior design isn't required. This is great because most programs require you to have a background in interior design in order to get your masters.

When you were in high school, how important was education to you?
Education was very important. In school I got straight As, I paid attention in class, I studied, I did my homework... I was very self-motivated even though it seemed as if it made me an outcast for actually raising my hand and getting good grades. I remember once getting an A on a paper, and someone looked at me in complete disgust and said, "you think you are better than everyone else, huh?" People look down on you when you are doing well, but for some reason I never let that get to me and continued to push myself.

Do you think education as important now?
Education, especially for interior design is important. People take interior designers very seriously because you have to go through this process and get your education, otherwise no one will look at you as a professional. People have told me that maybe there is a back door into interior design-- maybe I didn't have to go back to school. The way I look at it, I am going to

be paying student loans the rest of my life regardless; I might as well be paying them off with doing what I love.

What are some of your proudest accomplishments?
I am always looking to do more and I am hard on myself. People look at the things I've done and are impressed, but I am not. I am always looking to get further ahead. When I sit and look at my life, yes, I've done pretty well... I've graduated with a bachelor's in mechanical engineering which is important to me because I am a black woman. There weren't many people like me in my class. Then I moved to California and am living on my own.

If interior design wasn't an option, what would you be doing instead?
I am big into fitness. Since I moved to California, I work out 4 times a week. I find places to go hiking, running the stairs, jogging by the beach. I am really big on motivating people to eat healthy and exercise and follow their dream. So I believe I would be really good as a fitness coach or motivational speaker.

What advice do you have for other young people who would like to be an interior designer like yourself?
The biggest obstacle that you'll have to face is yourself. You are the ruler of your fate. There are going to be so many people who try to bring you down just because you are trying to do good for yourself. None of those people matter, what does matter is your self-motivation and determination, your will to become better, to do more and to go further. You have to push yourself to work hard. Don't let anyone-- close friends, loved ones keep you from doing what's best for you.

Sateara Page

Picture Perfect Inside and Out

Sateara: I am an image consultant, personal shopper, wardrobe stylist and extreme organizer. I wardrobe style and give creative insight for photoshoots, special events/occasions, and makeovers, as well as personal image branding. I feel as though when a person sees your image on the outside, it is a direct reflection on what goes on the inside. In the midst of all these superficial fixes, I focus on motivating my clients and encouraging. I constantly remind them how beautiful or handsome they are.

When you were young what did you want to grow up and become?
When I was young I vividly remember wanting to be an mechanical engineer. I absolutely love working with my hands and I like to try to fix things.

When you were in high school, how important was education to you?
Education was very important to me in high school. Education is as important, if not more important now because I have an 8 year old who is so precious to me. She deserves to have a mother who practices what she preaches. I call her "Dr. London Renee Page"

daily. I have an Associates in Business Administration. Soon, I would like to go to back to school for my next degree of Communications. My ultimate goal is to get my Doctorate in Divinity.

What are some of your most proud accomplishments?
Some of my most proud accomplishments was finishing high school on time while pregnant during my senior year of high school, giving birth to my beautiful child, and maintaining lifelong friendships.

What advice would you have for other young entrepreneurs who would like to start in the same field as yourself?
Stay connected to the fashion industry, be open minded, be kind, network and never be afraid to tell someone your vision... They might just buy into it.

For bookings or inquiries
 email: pointsofview07@yahoo.com

SERVICES:

- EDITING
- PROOF READING
- BUSINESS PROPOSAL
- BIOGRAPHY
- ESSAYS
- MAJOR REPORTS
- THESIS
- DISSERTATION
- BOOKS
- MANUSCRIPTS
- POEMS
- VOWS
- EULOGIES
- COVER LETTER
- RESUME

An Howard Publishing, a writing, editing and proofreading company. An Howard is also an author, she published her first collection of poetry, Whispers of Words Spoken May of 2012. This is the first of many books. Be on the look out for more from the desk of An Howard.

AN HOWARD PUBLISHING

Phone: 702-674-6282

Follow An Howard Publishing:

Twitter: @AnHoward1

FaceBook: An Howard Publishing

AnHowardPublishing.com

Nicci Gilbert

From songstress to fashion designer, R&B Diva, Nicci Gilbert shares her success story and lets B.O.S.S. inside her world of motivation, inspiration, and encouragement.

B.O.S.S.: You are one of the producers of the hit show R&B Divas. What was your inspiration for producing this show? What direction do you see the show going in?
Nicci: I created what has now become R&B Divas 10 years ago. I produced a musical called Soul Kittens Cabaret and I had the cast, which included Monifah, Angie Stone, and Syleena Johnson staying in a house together in Detroit. We filmed the ladies as they rehearsed and prepared for the musical and I knew then it would make a great docu-series to see the lives of these talented women unfold. I would like to see R&B Divas continue to brand talented performers and ultimately become bigger than "The Housewives Franchise".

Curvato Clothing is a clothing line you created to compliment women with curves. Please tell our readers how Curvato got its start. What was your motivation?
My motivation for Curvato was to empower women to embrace their curves and love themselves from the inside, out. I also feel that it's important for women to realize that curves can be complimented by the right clothing-- we don't have to hide our bodies. I started the line by simply creating clothing that I thought was flattering and fashionable and sharing the line with full-figured women. #LIVECURVY! (Laughs.)

What woman inspired you the most when you were growing up?

Why?
I have drawn inspiration from many women in my lifetime for many different reasons, but the woman who inspires me most is my mother, Helen Gilbert. My mother was the first entrepreneur that I knew… she owned houses, businesses, and instilled in us the drive to succeed. As a single parent, my mother brought home the bacon, fried, and served it. My mother also allowed us to be free thinkers, she taught us to never fear questioning the "status quo" and to choose our own paths in life.

Did you have a teacher who stood out in your life for going above the call of duty? Why?
The teacher who impacted my

"Surround yourself with people who love and encourage you, but who also keeps it real with you. "

life most was Susan Storey who I like to refer to as my "White Other Mother". (Laughs.) She was a drama teacher at Cody High School and if it had not been for her, I wouldn't have attended college on a theatre scholarship and I probably would not be a successful entertainer. Ms. Storey encouraged all of her students to maintain their GPAs and to put as much dedication into our passion for creative arts. Susan worked overtime and after hours with her students to prepare us for college and life after. My fondest memory of her is taking us to audition for our scholarships and when I fell short of a class I needed to qualify for a scholarship, she enrolled me in community college over the summer so I could attend Eastern Michigan University on the theatre scholarship in the fall.

What advice do you have for our readers who are interested in following a career path similar to yours?
I would advise anyone interested in pursuing a career in the entertainment industry to have very THICK SKIN, surround yourself with people who love and encourage you, but who also keeps it real with you. Lastly, and most importantly, read & understand every line of your contracts.

What is your motivation?
I'm motivated by my desire to inspire younger generations the way I was inspired by those before me. I would also like to leave a legacy that my loved ones can be proud of.

What projects are you working on that you want our readers to know about?
I am currently working on a few new docu-series... one of which is the 20 year reunion for Brownstone. I am launching my new digital channel www.noego.tv, working on a scripted series, and am also relaunching Curvato this Fall.
My Twitter/ Instagram and FB are ALLTHINGSNICCI

Education is so important. It helped me with basketball because if I didn't have my grades up, I couldn't play basketball. I knew it was important. I'm not going to lie, I wasn't an A student... I was an average "C" student. I was the type of student took a while to grasp things. Many kids think that some of their heroes were always the "greatest students" and then just became successful. But, no-- I had to work extra hard and there is nothing wrong with admitting that. You have weaknesses that may be someone else's strength and their strength may be someone else's weakness.

You have to find a niche-- find something you love. I was always into science. That's where I got my best grades, but I wasn't that good at math. I had to work extra hard in math because I knew I wasn't good at it. You just need that motivation to push you. I let basketball be that person to push me and keep me motivated in school. That's why I think students should have something that they are involved with as well to help push them through their education. Because let's be real, it's hard. It's hard to focus. But if they find that niche-- something they really love to do-- it can help give them that extra motivation to get through school. That's why I used basketball. I knew that if I didn't get the grades, I couldn't play and I knew I wanted to play. I started playing at 8 years old. Basketball motivated me. Even my parents... they were great parents even when they were pressuring me to do what I needed to do for school. As a kid, you are stubborn and don't want to listen. But I remember the first time my dad said, "If you don't get your grades up, you are not going to play basketball." I'll never forget that first time. I was like "oh my gosh. What do I have if you take basketball away from me?!" That was my source of fun and motivation. So I was like, I have to do something with these grades in order to keep playing.

Even if the kids don't choose basketball, there has to be something they can do. It's statistically proven that girls who are involved in extra-curricular activities are less likely to get pregnant at an early age and more likely to be successful in life and get a free education (scholarships) as far as college goes. So, whenever I speak to ladies I tell them, "please get involved in something." If you take notice, most of the girls who are pregnant early are not involved in a lot of activities, so they find time to do

other things. They wind up having kids at an early age and wishing later on that they would have done things differently. That's why I tell them that it doesn't matter if it's dancing, acting, sports, whatever… DO something. Find something you love and work hard at it.

B.O.S.S.: What was college like for you?

Angel: Science was big for me, then I discovered acting. Theatre became my major until it started to conflict with my basketball schedule. I switched majors a few times. I always tell students, don't get discouraged if you don't know what you want to be, everyone switches majors 2 to 3 times in their college career. Not knowing is ok. Stay focused.

They both (basketball and theatre) demand so much of your time, so I ended up switching my major to communication. The thing about college is that as a student athlete you need a strong support system that is set up by the school. They have everyone there who can possibly help you with what you may need. They give you tutors and academic assistants to help. But above that, you have your teammates… your sisterhood. It's not just basketball. Being on a team is like having 13 sisters that you know and love. You are always together, always on the road together, and you all have the same common goal. So to know that you have 13 other sisters with you pushing and lifting each other up that is so encouraging.

B.O.S.S.: How did the "sisterhood" help to motivate you?

Angel: [My teammates] definitely motivate me because you never want to let your teammates down. You never want to let your sister down. That's something we always brought up. Everyone played their role… some girls helped with studying one subject and others helped with another subject, and we just played off of each other's' weaknesses and strengths. So, it's like you have sisters who will help you and tutors and coaches who are more than willing to push you to succeed.

B.O.S.S.: What would you say to those girls who are struggling and don't have that strong support system?

Angel: You have to find the motivation within yourself. If you don't believe in yourself, no one else will. It's just one of those things where you say, I have to do it. If you can find good role models to look up to and learn from, watch them. What how they talk in interviews and interact with press. Read their story and see what they struggled with to get to where

When I was struggling and I wanted to quit, I didn't-- I just worked harder.

they are. People think the road to success is a straight line, but there are a lot of bumps and curves. So, read [your role model's] story-- you will learn a lot and say, "wow, I'm going through that too."

When it comes to giving back, what are some things you are involved with?

As far as volunteering, I know how important it is for someone to be educated and I take the time to give back to the youth and let them know to further their education. I try to teach them things I've learned through sports and real world stories.

I have my own organization called the Angel McCoughtry Dream Foundation. Just last month, we gave a group of students laptops for doing amazing book reports. Along with that, I also have a basketball camp coming up as well. When I go overseas to play in Turkey, I give back to the families in need. There are still a lot of communities there that are impoverished. So we give food during thanksgiving and gifts during Christmas.

What advice would you give to a student who was being bullied?

I was bullied. I was bullied because I was nice to everybody and people took advantage of that. I was "geekish," I guess, so a lot of people didn't want to hang around me. However, the thing about bullying is that you have to speak up. A lot of kids get bullied every day and they are holding it in and hurting. They decide to not say anything to a guardian or adult because they think it might not sound good or because they're scared. You have to speak up with any type of bullying so that the next step can take place.

I would also encourage the parents to look for the signs. You know your child and their emotions and attitudes, and if it changes, you have to find out why. So if your kid says, "I had a bad day in school," don't just say, " oh, it will get better tomorrow..." Find out why! It starts with telling someone. Don't be afraid to speak up.

If you werent' in basketball what would you be doing with your life instead?

I would be a music writer for big artists. Growing up I had no idea, I just recently figured that out... (Laughs.)

Who is the biggest inspiration in your life?

Oprah, Coretta Scott King, Betty

Shabazz, Myrlie Evers… They went through so much and made it through. Ladies like that really inspire me. To go through those things and still continue to fight and do things to help others, even into old age-- that inspires me.

Any final words of encouragement for the readers?

Let me tell you a story… my freshman year in college I just kept messing up and I couldn't get anything right. I kept being late for practice, I was late on the first day and I just couldn't get it together. I overheard my Head coach say, "buy her a plane ticket and send her home." I'll never forget that. It bothered me so much that he would give up on me like that. When I was struggling and I wanted to quit, I didn't-- I just worked harder. And, now, look what happened, I became the all-time leader in points for girls and boys basketball and I took that team further than they had ever been. They are even considering making a statue for me outside the stadium. (Laughs.) So never give up, never quit. Just work harder. In high school, I didn't past my SAT. I actually failed it really bad. I signed to go to St. John's University but I didn't qualify. I couldn't even get my diploma because I failed math class my senior year. It was like one of my worst years and I was a basketball star. On graduation day, I was sitting at home and my parents were disappointed in me but wouldn't say it. They had hurt in their eyes. From there, I decided to press on and go to junior college instead. That was another point where I wanted to give up, not play basketball, and not care. Just screw life, get a job, do whatever… But I begin to think and said, I should at least get my GED. So, I ended up going to a prep school in North Carolina. It made me focus and mature and I got my grades up and entered college. Sometimes things may not go the path you want it to go, but sometimes you have to go a different route. Sometimes you have to go down to get up and it's ok to take a different route. But what you can't do is give up. Even though I wanted to [give up] so bad… don't give up.

Tree's
Motivational
Corner

You Are Beautiful

A friend of mine asked me to help her with an event to mentor a group of girls from high school. Of course I jumped at the chance and was very excited about it. The event consisted of nine teenage girls, my friend and myself. I knew when I arrived that this was going to be a great evening of bonding and a great chance to help uplift more youth. One of the things we had the girls do was write down questions and put them in a cute little box. We wanted all questions to be anonymous. As we were going through questions we came across one that said, "I don't feel pretty and I don't like the way that I look. What should I do?" The entire room said, "Awwwwweee" in unison. As my friend started to speak on that question I began to glance around the room hoping to find the young lady that wrote that question. As I looked I did not see anyone who gave me any hints that it was them. My heart grew sad. When it was my turn to speak I said, "You are beautiful." I then proceeded to explain to the group that God makes us all unique and that we all have beautiful and wonderful attributes about us. We don't look like the person next to us, and that is a good thing. We need to love the person we see when we look in the mirror. Regardless of size, color, height, etc... there are things that we can do to enhance our beauty. Wear a nice outfit, do our hair nice, polish our nails, wear cute ear rings or a watch. Whatever

"Those are some of the things we can do on the outside, but on the inside is where most of the challenge occurs."

makes you feel great about yourself is what you need to do. Those are some of the things we can do on the outside, but on the inside is where most of the challenge occurs. Some teen are not getting the love they need from home, so they look for it in other places. It is sad, but a lot of our youth have issues at home. This is why I encourage youth to find a hobby. Having an outlet is a great way to keep their minds off of negative issues and on to positive ones. Excelling at a hobby will always make us feel good about ourselves.

I encouraged the young lady to come and talk to me outside of the group because I am great at boosting confidence and self-esteem in girls and women. Even though she has not reached out to me yet, I am hoping that one day she will. It is important for young girls to look in the mirror and tell themselves You Are Beautiful, but more importantly for them to believe it!

By: LaTresa "Tree" Cunningham
Twitter: @PurpleDiva13

Award Winning Chicago Deep Dish Pizza!
PLUS, TRADITIONAL & SUPER THIN PIZZA CRUST STYLES!
"Best Stuffed Pizza in Chicago!"
Authentic Chicago Deep Dish
Chicago's
Nancy's Pizza™
• APPETIZERS
• SALADS
• SANDWICHES
• NEW PERSONAL SIZE DEEP DISH PIZZA!
• TRY A NANCY'S SIGNATURE PIZZA!
KARAOKE
EVERY FRIDAY
& SATURDAY NIGHT
9PM 'TIL 1AM!
WE CATER
SMALL & LARGE EVENTS!
DELIVERY AVAILABLE!
ATLANTA • 3167 Peachtree Rd NE in Buckhead • 404-842-9997

Tonda
Peterson-Bryant
Create your own Path!

B.O.S.S.: B.O.S.S. stands for "Be your Own Success Story." Tell me, what does being successful and being a "boss" mean to you?

Tonda: For me, being successful means that you are doing something that is fulfilling. It makes you happy, not necessarily making big bucks, but you are happy doing it.

Being a boss means that you are able to create your own path, you decide what it is you want to do and you make it happen. It is something you can do alone or with others who can help you accomplish your goal. Just making whatever needs to happen, happen...that is what being a boss means to me.

B.O.S.S.: As an entrepreneur, tell us about your company and what motivated you to start it.

Tonda: I am a teacher by trade, having taught special education for almost 8 years. During that time, my brother was in the NBA and he needed help with day to day things so that he could focus on basketball. He asked me to work for him and I did. I handled his day to day errands-- paying bills, getting his car serviced or washed... I noticed that some of the other guys on his team didn't have someone like that. They were either trying to handle their own business or they had someone who wasn't doing a good job at it. During the later part of my brother's career, I started thinking about whether or not I would go back to teaching once his we reached the end of his career. I wasn't sure about what I would do. I saw that there was a need for what I was doing and that's how "Special T Concierge" came to be.

B.O.S.S.: What advice would you have for youth interested in pursuing a career in concierge service?

Tonda: I would say that you have to be a giver. You do a lot more than just what the clients need. It's trying to figure out what they need and go above and beyond their expectations. You must have a giving heart, be self-motivated, and be imaginative all wrapped up in one.

B.O.S.S.: When you were in school, who was your favorite teacher and how did they impact your life?

Tonda: A teacher by the name of Mrs. Abrey... she was one on my teachers in elementary school. She had a way to make me feel like I can do anything I set my mind to. Even though my parents always instilled that in me, hearing it from someone else

"I want them to know you can accomplish whatever you set your mind to. Don't ever let anyone tell you that your dream is unattainable."

impacts you differently. She was very encouraging. If I ever made a mistake she would explain why the mistake was made and how to correct it. Mrs. Abrey genuinely cared for her students outside of being a teacher. That always stuck with me throughout my life

B.O.S.S.: I know you are an athlete, what sports did you play growing up and how do you believe participating in them has benefited you today?

Tonda: I played volleyball, basketball , softball, track, and cross country. Seems like I've tried everything! My two major ones were basketball and volleyball. I did track and cross country to stay in shape for the others sports. They all definitely made an impact on me. Playing a team sport teaches you how to rely on and work with other people. It also taught me about being competitive. In the real world, you have to know what you want, be willing to work for what you want, stay focused and win. So, I believe sports definitely helped me be the person I am and what it is I am doing right now.

B.O.S.S.: What is the last piece of advice you have for our readers?

Tonda: I want them to know you can accomplish whatever you set your mind to. Don't ever let anyone tell you that your dream is unattainable. Just keep God first and stay focused. There will always be naysayers and people will always try to discourage you. But if you believe in your heart that this is what you are supposed to do and that you want to do,then you can absolutely do it. You have to be willing to work hard for it... nothing is going to be easy, so make sure you stay focused on what you are trying to accomplish.

Special T Concierge
www.specialtconcierge.com
twitter: IamSpecial_T

HBCU &U

Why I chose an HBCU.

"Historically black colleges and universities are relevant in today's society because they empower the African-American community to seek higher education. We are encouraged to try new things and better ourselves to the point that not only will we be successful, but we will achieve excellence in whatever we do."

HBCUs will always be relevant because it gives us a sense of where we come from. They are perfect examples that there are educated black people who care about their future and want to be successful. My HBCU is really like a family from the professors to the students to the janitors who cleaned our dorm.

I initially chose an HBCU because of shows like A Different World and I thought that I would have a good time while getting a degree. Now, I stayed at an HBCU because I felt nurtured and that I was being prepared for a future with people who really wanted to see me succeed!

Dania Elise Ellington, *C/O 2007*

Johnson C. Smith University, Bachelor's of Fine Arts with a concentration in African-American Studies

I chose an HBCU because I wanted to be around people like me. I specifically chose Howard University because it was an HBCU that had a serious focus on my major and has a wonderful law school which I plan to attend. I actually decided to attend Howard when I was 8 years old. We get to do things like walk to the White House at 12 a.m. on Election Day because we took part in electing the first African-American president for a second term. Chanting and singing the whole way, it all reminded me of what our ancestors fought so hard for. The feeling I received from that was absolutely exhilarating. Experiences like that made my decision all the more worthwhile.

Nefertiti Robinson, *Junior*

Howard University, Political Science

HBCUs will be relevant as long as African-Americans are regarded as subpar individuals compared to their white counterparts. HBCUs give us the chance to "level out the playing field" and prepare us for a world where we must work harder and make greater achievements in order to be considered for certain positions. I chose to attend the illustrious Howard University because i felt it would better prepare me for a world where I will already be at a disadvantage based on my skin color.

Shane Lewis, *Junior*

Howard University, Audio Production

I think that HBCU's are very relevant in our society because they provide students of color the cultural and academic experiences needed to become productive citizens of our communities. They are also family oriented and one is able to really get personal, individual care and support from staff at a HBCU. Having attended a PWI for undergrad, the relationships, support, and need to go above and beyond was provided at an HBCU, whereas at the PWI it seemed more business oriented in which I was just another number.

I chose to attend a HBCU because a lot of our history is rooted in these institutions. I believe that we are some of the most intellectual people, and to gather together to share and gain knowledge is powerful. Lastly, I believe that the HBCU experience is one like no other that everyone should have a chance to experience.

Sanchaze Murray, *Summa Cum Laude C/O 2014*
Alabama State University, Masters of Education

Ten Job
Search Mistakes
New Grads Make

Written by:
Marcia Robinson,
http://www.thehbcucareercenter.com

By Marcia Robinson MBA, SPHR

Imagine the feeling you would get if you sent the wrong cover letter or resume to the wrong employer? Imagine hitting the submit key before you attached a transcript or completed the online job application? All of these job search errors happen every day, because everybody makes job search mistakes. Some job search mistakes are easier than others to correct. For example, if you sent the wrong cover letter, you can very quickly send an update. Some job search mistakes, however, when repeated over and over can have a detrimental effect and will stand between you and a job offer you really want. Many of the following job search mistakes new graduates make can be avoided with a little bit of research and preparation.

Bad resumes and cover letters

1. This is a no brainer. AOL jobs reports that 61% of resumes have typos and errors. There are so many free resume samples and cover letter samples available for free on the internet, there is no excuse to have a bad resume or cover letter. Find a layout and format you like, write your résumé and get it critiqued by a career coach, a human resources manager, a professional recruiter or contact the career center on the campus where you graduated. More than 95% of college career centers work with their new grads after commencement.

2. Digital dirt is all over your social media

Too many new graduates forget to clean up their profiles, or what I like to call digital dirt online. Twitter bios and timelines, Facebook pages etc. should all be stripped of any negative information that could cause a recruiter to dismiss you as a candidate. New grads who make this mistake often are not aware that what they are doing is driving recruiters away.

3. Stop talking college major and start talking job skills

New grads sometimes forget that they need to do more than talk about their college degree or their college major. Actual job skills, experience, internships, accomplishments, leadership and career goals must now become a part of your conversations. Doing mock interviews will definitely help a new professional learn how to infuse good stories about great outcomes in a job interview.

4. Hiding from networking

In a digital economy, some job seekers believe that posting a resume on a niche job board is all they need to do in a job search. Not true. Yes, new graduates must have an online job search strategy, but they must also have an "on-land" strategy. Move away from the computer and meet actual people at job fairs, community or campus events, professional association meetings or social arrangements like Meet-ups. As Marc Williams, CEO of Williams Communications LLC and professional development coach to college athletes, says all the time, "It is not who YOU know. It's who knows YOU." Connecting with people professionally online is sometimes only possible when you have learned how to connect with people in person. See the 10 Tips for Winning a Room

5. Not following up

Whether it's with a job lead, a networking contact or a personal referral, new graduates struggle in the job search without consistent effort and follow up. Time is of the essence when following up and new grads must act with a sense of urgency.

6. Poor interview performance

If new grads are failing in the job search because of poor interview performance, a mock interview could be the answer. Practice interviews will help new grads develop their ability to answer questions and stay confident in the job interview. Remember my 3 C's of Interviewing: grew excellent COMMUNICATION skills to speak with CONFIDENCE about your COMPETENCIES.

7. Not using the college career center

National Association of Colleges and Employers reports that 72% of graduating college seniors who plan to enter the workforce, use the college career center. From my personal experience in career centers, the percentage of African American students using these services before graduation is about 30%. Greater use of this valuable service will definitely yield greater job search success.

8. Don't know what employers want

This is a major job search roadblock for new grads and yet it is one of the easiest issues to address. Every year employers share the skills they want from new graduates through surveys. Find out these in-demand skills and make them the focus of your resume and your interview. You can always find them on our web site.

9. Lack of research

After 15 years working with new professionals, this is biggest complaint employers would make about new graduates during the on-campus interview process. Too many new grads do absolutely no research on the job, the company or the industry. In the recruiter's mind, this lack of research shows up as a lack of interest.

10. No mentors or career advisors

Personal mentors and career advisors play a critical role in a successful new graduate job search strategy. These are the professionals who help new grads understand possible career paths, find out about job leads, help explore options and evaluate job opportunities and job offers.

Three

Section 3

Dr. Adrienne Johnson

When you were a teenager what did you want to be when you grew up?

Well, I wanted to be a track star and I knew I wanted to be a professional. But, I didn't know what that meant. When I was growing up, being a "professional" meant you either worked for the government or you were a school teacher. I knew there had to be more to it than that. You didn't see a lot of black entrepreneurs except doctors and lawyers, but I wasn't too interested in those professions. I used to look at the magazines like Jet and Ebony and I'd look at the advertisements that had black "professionals" dressed in suits and carrying a briefcase, and I knew that's what I wanted to be. I didn't know where they were going or what they were doing, but I knew I wanted to be that.

Did you follow any specific steps in order to reach that goal?

I knew that in order to be a professional you had to have a degree. So, I knew I had to go to college and I had to get a degree. But things did not work out that simply. Dr. Johnson's parents were not rich, but to achieve her goals she had to go to college and do whatever it took to graduate- no excuses. Her motivation, she saw it in her parents, she saw it in her aunts and uncles, and their friends. All college graduates, all successful. There was no other option.

What happened after you started college?

I majored in Sociology. One day, my father was speaking to me and asked, "You are smart, and you make great grades, why are you majoring in Sociology?" I told him, because I wanted to help people. And he said something that changed my life... he said, "If you really want to help people, major in Business. Go to the School of Business. Get a job and make a lot of money so you can help all the people you want." And he was exactly right.

Dr. Johnson comes from a long line of people helping people. From watching her grandmother who was a "domestic" do for others in the community to her mother who was an avid volunteer. Dr. Johnson has witnessed her share of altruism. "I'm from the south," she says. "I carry a sermon in my purse."

B.O.S.S.: What lead you to become an entrepreneur?

My father instilled in us that it is very important to own your OWN. That way, you don't have to worry about getting pink slips or being fired. If you own your own business, education, degree, money, you control your own destiny. I learned early on that entrepreneurship was the way to go. I worked full- time in the day to make money to support my son because I was a single mother. Then, at night, I worked at my own company part-time. I owned a Public Relations company, but really it was just me. I needed income and working two or three jobs outside of home wasn't an option for me because I was raising my child myself. My "in-house" PR Company provided an opportunity that didn't take away from my son.

You began your journey as an entrepreneur as a part-time endeavor.

How did you transition into doing it full-time?

I didn't go into full- time self-employment until after I retired from Coca-Cola after 23 years of service. The Coke Company was a great opportunity because I learned so much. I learned great marketing and business skills from all the meetings and programs. All the experience, contacts, and classes helped me to translate [what I learned] over to my own company. [Coca-Cola] trains you well. I retired in March of 2011 and I started my business two weeks later. I definitely didn't wait long. I just kept thinking, "God has too much for me to do... too much in store for me." And I really wanted to begin helping people.

Along with my PR Company, I also put together a business etiquette training course for the youth. There were a lot of young people interviewing at Coke and when we took them to lunch they would blow the interview, during lunch. Remember, the interview doesn't end until you get in your car and go home. They didn't know what to do with their napkins didn't know what conversation to have, didn't know how to properly behave and they were losing out on their opportunity because of it.

I also specialize in motivational speaking. How to motivate someone going from ordinary to extraordinary, how to become successful, how to persevere, how never to give up, how to be empowered, how to be prepared. Being prepared means knowing a second language or getting a higher degree. It is important to go on. Being committed to the job no matter how small it is or how you think it insignificant. Lastly, I talk to students about going global, taking them from U.S. to Africa and vice versa. You need global experience in today's work place.

How much of your success would you credit to Luck?

Luck has nothing to do with it. I always tell my students that HOPE IS NOT A STRATEGY! When you talk to people they always say "I hope to become a lawyer, or I hope to become a doctor, or executive." Well, hope is not a strategy-- you have to plan and be prepared. 100% was my faith in God. God will open and close doors that man can do nothing about. The other part is NETWORKING. People give to PEOPLE and people hire PEOPLE. So when you go into these interviews or into these meetings, you have to show people YOU and why you are different from everyone else, not what's on [your resume].

Looking back, do you think you've made the right decisions for your life?
I think the path I took was a hard path, being a teenage mother. But, the path I took was the path that was there for me. I was dreaming big dreams. There are three types of people that you have to have that are very important in being successful. Mentors, people who talk to you. Coaches, those are people who talk with you. And finally sponsors, those are people who talk for you. Many of the opportunities you have will be determined when you are not in the room, so you have to develop sponsors to speak for you when you're not in the room.

"I think the path I took was a hard path, being a teenage mother. But, the path I took was the path that was there for me. "

Adrienne Booth Johnson, the CEO of Infinity Global Connections, LLC., has delivered hundreds of lectures, seminars, commencement and keynote speeches for colleges, major corporations and non-profit organizations. Recent speaking engagements include Livingstone College (Salisbury, NC), Kentucky State University (Frankfort, KY), Talladega College (Talladega, AL) and Southern University (New Orleans, LA). In May 2011 she was awarded an honorary Doctor of Divinity Degree at from St. Paul College (Lawrenceville, VA).

Adrienne earned a Certificate of Divinity at the Interdenominational Theological Center (ITC) in Atlanta and was licensed as a Minister in 2008. She is an Associate Minister at Zion Hill Baptist Church in Atlanta, GA. Additionally, she is an international missionary who works with ministers, women and children in rural villages of Durban, Johannesburg and Cape Town, South Africa. She has also preached in Nairobi, Kenya, and has visited Liberia and Ghana. She also created the Young Women's Entrepreneur Program in Monrovia Liberia, in conjunction with the Liberia Coca-Cola Bottling Company. In which 40 Liberian women became Coca-Cola vendors. As a result of Adrienne's initiative, the program has now expanded to over 500 women, with a goal of 1500 women.

A graduate of the University of Louisville's School of Business, Adrienne is a high-energy speaker whose enthusiasm is contagious. She was employed by The Coca-Cola Company for more than 22 years. Her passion is working with all college students but particularly Historically Black Colleges and Universities (HBCU). Of special note is her execution of the 2010 World Cup in the African American community when she accompanied 21 HBCU students to Johannesburg, South Africa on the "Coca-Cola Open Happiness Tour" to the 2010 World Cup.

Adrienne co-authored a book entitled, Do's and Don'ts of Fundraising, a practical guide to successful fundraising, along with her husband, Attorney Joseph Johnson, and her friend, Mrs. Suzanne Mayo-Theus. The book draws on their personal wealth of business wisdom to show churches and organizations how essential fundamental fundraising skills can apply to real life challenges. She also started a second business. She opened Adrienne's Fine Resale Boutique in Atlanta (Buckhead) on May 31, 2013. Adrienne's Is an upscale consignment store " where luxury meets affordability".

Her extensive community involvement includes membership in: The Links, Inc, Magnolia Chapter; Trustee of the Foundations Board for Jack and Jill of America, Inc.; Board of Directors for The House of Dawn Teen Pregnancy Program; President's Advisory Board of Livingstone College; Beta Epsilon Chapter of Alpha Kappa Alpha Sorority; Fundraising Board of Athletes Against Drugs; and founder, organizer and first president of the Lake Spivey Chapter of Jack and Jill of America, Inc.

Adrienne Booth Johnson lives in Fayetteville, GA, with her husband, Attorney Joseph Johnson. They have two children, Attorney Bill Green and Jayla Amani Johnson. They have three grandchildren, Taylor, Will and Ethan.

Youth Health Summit at
University of North Carolina Wilmington

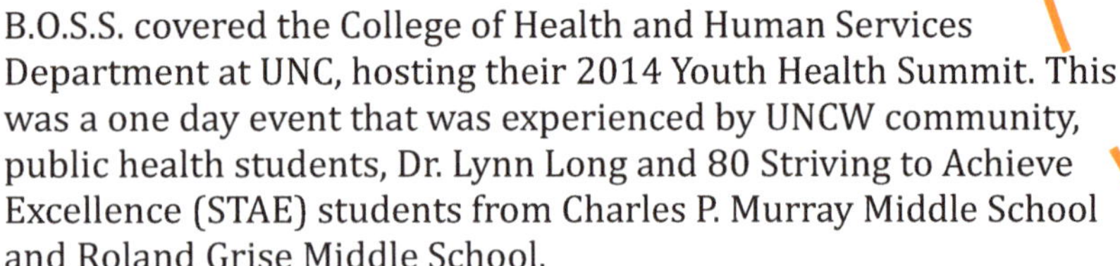

B.O.S.S. covered the College of Health and Human Services Department at UNC, hosting their 2014 Youth Health Summit. This was a one day event that was experienced by UNCW community, public health students, Dr. Lynn Long and 80 Striving to Achieve Excellence (STAE) students from Charles P. Murray Middle School and Roland Grise Middle School.

University students taught sessions to STAE students on these 4 primary topics:

*Body image, nutrition/physical activity
*Stress management
*Screen time- bullying and cyber bulling
*Tobacco use prevention

After the sessions, participants were met outside by Sammie the Seahawk, UNCW's mascot who took pictures with everyone. With the school's executive chef and sous chef, a healthy food demonstration was presented to the students for lunch. Several students said they have never eaten squash before and were surprised by the healthy menu choices. The middle school students enjoyed interacting with university students who sat at each table. The younger students were able to ask them questions about college, their goals, how they worked to get there, and what they liked to do.

Afterwards, the Dean of Health and Human Services, Dr. Charles Hardy met with the students and gave them words of encouragement. Also, the New Hanover County Health Department donated speedometers for each student to track their physical activity.

A lot of the students expressed that peers in their schools were cutting themselves. We (UNCW) wanted them to really understand that there are healthy ways to manage stress. During the nutrition activities, we showed them how much sugar was in soda. They were very surprised at the amount that is in a 20oz can of soda and how much sugar they were ingesting in a day with sweetened drinks. Also, the topic of cyber bullying was prevalent. They thought they'd post something for two seconds and it disappear and didn't realize the effects it had on others.

All in all, the day seemed to be a success with the participants learning so much information and interacting with the University.

Spelman Women of Color Leadership Conference 2014

By: Desha "DrDesha" Elliott

Spelman College celebrated their 10th Anniversary of their annual Leadership and Women of Color Leadership Conference. Themed "21st Century Leadership: Leading Forward, the conference covered key essentials for success in the workplace and in one's personal life. Topics covered were diversity, innovation, workplace game changing strategies, the blueprint for how to be a phenomenal leader for the next decade, and many more. Expertise from women from various background and fields created a rich atmosphere for learning at every session. In essence the foundation for the conference can be summarized best by these two outstanding leaders:

"If you are not seated at the table, then you are what's on the menu."- Major General Marcia Anderson, first African American woman Major General in the U.S. Army Reserve

"Whether it is corporate America, on the block, half way around the world in China, define yourself, know who you are. If you believe in yourself, you are insistent, you will be respected and you have yourself prepared, you will make your own way."

-Paula Madison, Retired NBC Universal Chief Diversity Office and multimillion dollar business woman

"Education has been everything for my career because there are certain things that will make you stand out and have longevity, not only in this (entertainment) industry but in many industries- that is your education. One of the things about going to Spelman, it was a Liberal Arts College and it taught you a lot about a lot of different things. It gave me a well-rounded education that served me later on in my career. I was able to use many of the lessons I learned here at Spelman throughout the rest of my career, and hopefully I am still using them, and will still be able to use them for many years to come. Education is the key. Many people think that they can get along without it, and yeah some people can, but you don't ever regret going to school and getting a degree." – Shaun Robinson, Emmy Award Winning Journalist and Access Hollywood Host